Fancy Coleslaw Recipes

Better and Tastier Ways to Make Coleslaw

By: Tyler Sweet

© 2022 Tyler Sweet, All Rights Reserved.

License Page

This book or any of its content may not be replicated by any means. Copying, publishing, distributing the contents of this publication without the explicit permission of the author is an infringement of the country's copyright law and will leave you liable to litigation. The contents of this book are well researched and fact-checked before printing to ensure that the readers get the best value. The author is not liable or responsible for the wrongful use of the information provided in the contents of this book.

Table of Contents

Introduction 5

1. Classic Coleslaw with A Punch 6

2. Creamy Red Cabbage Coleslaw 8

3. Caribbean Coleslaw 10

4. Herbed and Extra Creamy Coleslaw 13

5. Southern-Style Coleslaw 15

6. Zesty Coleslaw 17

7. 4-Ingredient Coleslaw 19

8. Red Wine Vinegar Coleslaw 21

9. No Mayo Coleslaw 23

10. Pickled Coleslaw 25

11. Celeriac Coleslaw 27

12. Seedy Coleslaw 29

13. Parmesan Cream Coleslaw 31

14. Fennel and Red Cabbage Coleslaw 33

15. Prawn Coleslaw 35

16. Sweet and Sour Coleslaw ... 38

17. Spicy Mango Coleslaw ... 41

18. Pickled Chili Coleslaw ... 43

19. Waldorf Coleslaw ... 45

20. Chili Peanut Coleslaw ... 47

21. Buttermilk Coleslaw ... 49

22. Almond Coleslaw ... 51

23. Pineapple Coleslaw ... 53

24. Tahini Coleslaw ... 55

25. Mediterranean Coleslaw ... 57

26. Spicy Avocado Coleslaw ... 60

27. Beetroot Coleslaw ... 62

28. Tahini Turkey Coleslaw ... 64

29. Apricot Coleslaw ... 67

30. Mexican Coleslaw ... 69

Conclusion ... 71

Biography ... 72

Author's Note ... 73

Introduction

No more boring coleslaw y'all.

The reputation of coleslaw being wobbly, merely enticing, and not tasty is over. Right here, we give coleslaw fantastic facelifts that would change your love for coleslaw for the better.

Simple ingredients can boost coleslaw that would make you love this salad like never before. So, we assembled thirty mind-blowing ones that would make you enjoy coleslaw better and more often.

Do you want to check them out? Wait no further.

1. Classic Coleslaw with A Punch

This coleslaw is the classic that we know about but doesn't leave the dressing at mayonnaise only. It adds a punch in celery seeds, apple cider vinegar, and sweetener for a better taste and flavor.

Prep Time: 15 mins

Serves: 4

Ingredients:

Slaw:

- ½ small green cabbage, outer leaves removed and shredded
- ½ small red cabbage, outer leaves removed and shredded
- 3 medium carrots, peeled and shredded
- ½ cup coarsely chopped parsley leaves

Dressing:

- 1 cup mayonnaise
- 2 tbsp Dijon mustard
- 1 tsp celery seeds
- 2 tbsp apple cider vinegar or to taste
- Salt and black pepper to taste
- 1 to 2 tsp honey, maple syrup, or sugar or to taste

Instructions:

Add all the slaw ingredients to a bowl.

In a bowl, mix the dressing ingredients until smooth.

Drizzle half of the dressing on the slaw and mix until well combined.

Add more of the dressing as desired and mix well.

Serve the coleslaw immediately or chilled.

2. Creamy Red Cabbage Coleslaw

Red cabbage has enough character by itself that it will shine on any platter. So, by making a creamy bunch, you create a simple but delicious slaw.

Prep Time: 15 mins

Serves: 4

Ingredients:

Slaw:

- 1 small red cabbage, outer leaves and shredded
- 1 large carrot, peeled and shredded
- 1 small red onion, shredded or very thinly sliced
- 1 large celery stalks, shredded

Dressing:

- ¾ cup mayonnaise
- 1 tbsp apple cider vinegar or to taste
- 2 tbsp fresh lemon juice or to taste
- Salt and black pepper to taste

Instructions:

Add all the slaw ingredients to a bowl.

In a bowl, mix the dressing ingredients until smooth.

Drizzle half of the dressing on the slaw and mix until well combined.

Add more of the dressing as desired and mix well.

Serve the coleslaw immediately or chilled.

3. Caribbean Coleslaw

Adding some mangoes, pineapple, and papayas to standard coleslaw would make you want to eat this slaw by itself and even more of it.

Prep Time: 15 mins

Serves: 4

Ingredients:

Slaw:

- ½ small green cabbage, outer leaves removed and shredded
- ½ small red cabbage, outer leaves removed and shredded
- 3 green onions, finely chopped
- ¼ cup chopped fresh parsley
- 1 small pineapple, peeled, cored, and finely cubed
- 2 large mangoes, peeled and finely cubed
- 2 large papayas, peeled, deseeded and finely cubed
- ½ cup sliced almonds

Dressing:

- 2 tbsp Dijon mustard
- 3 tbsp honey
- 1 tbsp red wine
- 2 tbsp fresh lemon juice
- 1 to 1 ½ tsp hot sauce
- 2 tbsp olive oil
- 2 tbsp brown sugar
- 1 tsp pureed garlic
- ½ jalapeno pepper, deseeded and minced

Instructions:

Add all the slaw ingredients to a bowl.

In a bowl, mix the dressing ingredients until smooth.

Drizzle half of the dressing on the slaw and mix until well combined.

Add more of the dressing as desired and mix well.

Serve the coleslaw immediately or chilled.

4. Herbed and Extra Creamy Coleslaw

You can buy a premade coleslaw mix at the store to save you the shredding time. Toss in some herbs and make the dressing extra creamy using heavy cream.

Prep Time: 15 mins

Serves: 4

Ingredients:

Slaw:

- 14 ounces bag coleslaw mix
- 1 tsp finely chopped chives
- 1 tsp finely chopped parsley

Dressing:

- 1 cup mayonnaise
- 1 tsp prepared yellow mustard
- 2 tbsp heavy cream
- Garlic salt and black pepper to taste

Instructions:

Add all the slaw ingredients to a bowl.

In a bowl, mix the dressing ingredients until smooth.

Drizzle half of the dressing on the slaw and mix until well combined.

Add more of the dressing as desired and mix well.

Serve the coleslaw immediately or chilled.

5. Southern-Style Coleslaw

This Southern coleslaw maintains the standard ingredients used in making coleslaw and boosts its tastes with some pickled dressing than merely mayonnaise.

Prep Time: 15 mins

Serves: 4

Ingredients:

Slaw:

- ⅔ small green cabbage, outer leaves removed and shredded
- ¼ small red cabbage, outer leaves removed and shredded
- 2 medium carrots, peeled and shredded
- 1 celery stalk, finely chopped

Dressing:

- ½ cup mayonnaise
- 2 tbsp sweet pickle relish
- ¼ cup sweet pickle juice
- ½ tsp celery seeds
- 2 tsp sugar or to taste, optional
- Salt to taste

Instructions:

Add all the slaw ingredients to a bowl.

In a bowl, mix the dressing ingredients until smooth.

Drizzle half of the dressing on the slaw and mix until well combined.

Add more of the dressing as desired and mix well.

Serve the coleslaw immediately or chilled.

6. Zesty Coleslaw

Let your coleslaw give you a nice zing by adding a comfortable bunch of lemon zest.

Prep Time: 15 mins

Serves: 4

Ingredients:

Slaw:

- ½ small green cabbage, outer leaves removed and shredded
- ½ small red cabbage, outer leaves removed and shredded
- 1 small red bell pepper, deseeded and finely chopped
- 1 small yellow bell pepper, deseeded and finely chopped
- ¼ small sweet onion, peeled and shredded

Dressing:

- 1 cup mayonnaise
- 3 tbsp apple cider vinegar
- ½ tsp celery seeds
- 1 tsp fresh lemon zest
- ⅓ cup sugar
- Salt and black pepper to taste

Instructions:

Add all the slaw ingredients to a bowl.

In a bowl, mix the dressing ingredients until smooth.

Drizzle half of the dressing on the slaw and mix until well combined.

Add more of the dressing as desired and mix well.

Serve the coleslaw immediately or chilled.

7. 4-Ingredient Coleslaw

With just 4 ingredients, you can make delicious coleslaw that isn't boring. Check out how.

Prep Time: 15 mins

Serves: 4

Ingredients:

Slaw:

- 1 ⅔ cups coleslaw mix

Dressing:

- ½ cup mayonnaise
- 1 ½ tbsp apple cider vinegar
- 1 ½ tbsp honey or sugar or to taste
- Salt to taste, optional

Instructions:

Add all the slaw mix to a bowl.

In a bowl, mix the dressing ingredients until smooth.

Drizzle half of the dressing on the slaw and mix until well combined.

Add more of the dressing as desired and mix well.

Serve the coleslaw immediately or chilled.

8. Red Wine Vinegar Coleslaw

By simply tossing red wine vinegar with coleslaw, you elevate its flavor while sparing out the creamy feel for a healthier option.

Prep Time: 15 mins

Serves: 4

Ingredients:

Slaw:

- ⅔ small red cabbage, outer leaves removed and shredded
- ⅓ small red cabbage, outer leaves removed and shredded
- 2 carrots, peeled and shredded

Dressing:

- 3 tbsp red wine vinegar
- 2 tbsp extra virgin olive oil
- 1 tbsp granulated sugar
- Salt and black pepper to taste

Instructions:

Add all the slaw ingredients to a bowl.

In a bowl, mix the dressing ingredients until smooth.

Drizzle half of the dressing on the slaw and mix until well combined.

Add more of the dressing as desired and mix well.

Serve the coleslaw immediately or chilled.

9. No Mayo Coleslaw

This no mayo coleslaw is a nice twist to enjoy some slaw with vinaigrette while keeping things simple.

Prep Time: 15 mins

Serves: 4

Ingredients:

Slaw:

- 1 ⅔ cups coleslaw mix

Dressing:

- ½ cup white distilled vinegar
- ¼ cup granulated white sugar
- Salt and black pepper to taste

Instructions:

Add all the coleslaw mix to a bowl.

In a bowl, mix the dressing ingredients until smooth.

Drizzle half of the dressing on the slaw and mix until well combined.

Add more of the dressing as desired and mix well.

Serve the coleslaw immediately or chilled.

10. Pickled Coleslaw

You would not be able to resist this coleslaw anytime, so our best advice is that you make plenty of it for multiple servings.

Prep Time: 27 mins

Cook Time: 1 min

Serves: 4

Ingredients:

Slaw:

- 3 cups thinly shredded green cabbage
- 1 cup matchstick carrots
- 3 radishes, cut into matchsticks

Pickle liquid:

- ½ cup unseasoned rice vinegar
- ½ cup water
- 1 tbsp granulated sugar
- 1 tbsp mustard seeds
- 1 ½ tsp salt

Instructions:

Add all the slaw ingredients to a bowl.

In a small saucepan, combine the pickle liquid ingredients and bring to a boil over high heat. Reduce the heat to low and let simmer for 1 minute. Stir until the sugar has dissolved.

Pour the pickle liquid over the cabbage mixture and stir until well-combined.

Chill uncovered for 10 to 12 minutes.

Drain and serve.

11. Celeriac Coleslaw

Celeriac is a low carb vegetable that is delicious and rarely used in meals. It substitutes nicely for cabbage and brings a different taste to your coleslaw servings.

Prep Time: 15 mins

Serves: 4

Ingredients:

Slaw:

- ½ celeriac, peeled and very thinly sliced
- 1 green apple, cored and thinly sliced or shredded
- 1 to 2 tbsp chopped fresh parsley

Dressing:

- 5 tbsp mayonnaise
- 1 tbsp Dijon mustard
- ½ lemon, juiced

Instructions:

Add all the slaw ingredients to a bowl.

In a bowl, mix the dressing ingredients until smooth.

Drizzle half of the dressing on the slaw and mix until well combined.

Add more of the dressing as desired and mix well.

Serve the coleslaw immediately or chilled.

12. Seedy Coleslaw

Toss some seeds of choice into coleslaw and add a lovely crunch to your servings. You don't get this much crunch with restaurant options.

Prep Time: 15 mins

Serves: 4

Ingredients:

Slaw:

- ½ small green cabbage, shredded
- 2 carrots, peeled and shredded
- 6 spring onions, trimmed and thinly sliced
- 2 tbsp toasted sunflower seed

Dressing:

- 2 tbsp plain yogurt
- 2 tbsp half and half
- 2 tsp wholegrain mustard
- 2 tsp olive oil
- 2 tsp white wine vinegar
- 2 tbsp orange juice
- Hemp seeds

Instructions:

Add all the slaw ingredients to a bowl.

In a bowl, mix the dressing ingredients until smooth.

Drizzle half of the dressing on the slaw and mix until well combined.

Add more of the dressing as desired and mix well.

Serve the coleslaw immediately or chilled.

13. Parmesan Cream Coleslaw

Parmesan on anything is always the best and by so, this coleslaw offers aromas that are the best.

Prep Time: 15 mins

Serves: 4

Ingredients:

Slaw:

- ½ small green cabbage
- 1 large carrot, peeled and shredded
- ½ medium red onion, peeled and thinly sliced
- ¼ cup thinly sliced fresh chives
- 3 tbsp mayonnaise

Dressing:

- 3 tbsp mayonnaise or plain yogurt
- 1 tsp Dijon mustard
- ¼ cup shredded Parmesan cheese

Instructions:

Add all the slaw ingredients to a bowl.

In a bowl, mix the dressing ingredients until smooth.

Drizzle half of the dressing on the slaw and mix until well combined.

Add more of the dressing as desired and mix well.

Serve the coleslaw immediately or chilled.

14. Fennel and Red Cabbage Coleslaw

Adding fennel to red cabbage replaces green cabbage in traditional coleslaw while boosting its flavor.

Prep Time: 15 mins

Serves: 4

Ingredients:

Slaw:

- ½ small red cabbage, outer leaves removed and shredded
- 1 fennel bulb, quartered and shredded
- 2 medium carrots, peeled and shredded
- ½ small red onion, shredded

Dressing:

- 3 tbsp mayonnaise or plain yogurt
- 1 tsp Dijon mustard

Instructions:

Add all the slaw ingredients to a bowl.

In a bowl, mix the dressing ingredients until smooth.

Drizzle half of the dressing on the slaw and mix until well combined.

Add more of the dressing as desired and mix well.

Serve the coleslaw immediately or chilled.

15. Prawn Coleslaw

Who wouldn't want this coleslaw over the standard that is served? This version would make a nice presentation at any family or occasion dinner.

Prep Time: 15 mins

Cook Time: 2 to 3 mins

Serves: 4

Ingredients:

Slaw:

- 1 cup prawns, deveined and peeled
- Salt to taste
- ½ small green cabbage, outer leaves removed and shredded
- 1 large carrot, peeled and shredded
- 1 radish, thinly sliced
- 2 handfuls beansprouts
- 2 tbsp coarsely chopped fresh cilantro

Dressing:

- 1 lime, zested and juiced
- 1 tbsp sesame oil
- 1 tsp ginger paste
- 2 tsp sugar
- 1 red chili, deseeded and minced

Instructions:

Season prawns with salt and steam in a steamer or pot for 2 to 3 minutes or until pink and opaque. Drain and set aside.

Add all the slaw ingredients to a bowl.

In a bowl, mix the dressing ingredients until smooth.

Drizzle half of the dressing on the slaw and mix until well combined.

Add more of the dressing as desired and mix well.

Place the prawns on the coleslaw.

Serve.

16. Sweet and Sour Coleslaw

A bit of sweetness and a bit of sourness can turn your standard coleslaw into a thing of much pleasure.

Prep Time: 15 mins

Serves: 4

Ingredients:

Slaw:

- ½ small green cabbage, outer leaves removed and shredded
- 2 carrots, peeled and thinly sliced
- 1 medium red bell pepper, deseeded and thinly sliced
- 1 small red onion, shredded
- 1 celery stalk, thinly sliced
- 8 radishes, thinly sliced

Dressing:

- 2 tbsp white wine vinegar
- ½ lemon, juiced
- 4 tbsp vegetable oil
- 1 tsp mustard powder
- 2 tbsp brown sugar
- ½ tsp yellow mustard seeds
- ½ tsp celery seeds

Instructions:

Add all the slaw ingredients to a bowl.

In a bowl, mix the dressing ingredients until smooth.

Drizzle half of the dressing on the slaw and mix until well combined.

Add more of the dressing as desired and mix well.

Serve the coleslaw immediately or chilled.

17. Spicy Mango Coleslaw

This coleslaw is a balance between mango salsa and mango salad. It settles somewhere in between nicely and would go so well with meat dishes.

Prep Time: 15 mins

Serves: 4

Ingredients:

- ½ small white cabbage, outer leaves removed and shredded
- ½ white radish, cut into thin matchsticks
- 1 mango, peeled and chopped
- 1 small red bell pepper, deseeded and cut into thin matchsticks
- 1 green chili, deseeded and minced
- A small handful cilantro, roughly chopped
- 1 lime, juiced

Instructions:

Add all the ingredients to a bowl.

Toss until well-combined.

Serve.

18. Pickled Chili Coleslaw

Throw some pickled red chilies into coleslaw to not only add some heat to it but also some tasty tang.

Prep Time: 15 mins

Serves: 4

Ingredients:

- 1 small red cabbage, outer leaves removed and shredded
- 3 medium carrots, shredded
- 1 red onion, thinly sliced
- 2 tbsp pickled red chilies, deseeded and minced
- 1 lime, juiced

Instructions:

Add all the ingredients to a bowl.

Toss until well-combined.

Serve.

19. Waldorf Coleslaw

This traditional coleslaw is rich with green apples, celery, walnuts, and a simple vinegar dressing. It is sweet, tangy, punchy in flavor, crunchy, and nutty.

Prep Time: 15 mins

Serves: 4

Ingredients:

Slaw:

- 1 small white cabbage, outer leaves removed and shredded
- 2 green apples, peeled and shredded
- 4 sticks celery, thinly sliced
- A handful of red or green grapes, halved
- A small handful of walnuts, toasted and chopped

Dressing:

- 6 tbsp light mayonnaise
- 1 tbsp white wine vinegar

Instructions:

Add all the slaw ingredients to a bowl except for the walnuts.

In a bowl, mix the dressing ingredients until smooth.

Drizzle half of the dressing on the slaw and mix until well combined.

Add more of the dressing as desired and mix well.

Sprinkle the walnuts on top and serve the coleslaw immediately or chilled.

20. Chili Peanut Coleslaw

You elevate the Asian-ness of coleslaw when you make it this way. Its amazing flavor bursts from afar and the chew is just heartwarming.

Prep Time: 15 mins

Serves: 4

Ingredients:

Slaw:

- ½ small green cabbage, outer leaves removed and shredded
- 1 large carrot, peeled and shredded
- 1 red onion, shredded
- A handful of cilantro, coarsely chopped
- 1 to 2 tsp toasted peanuts

Dressing:

- 1 tbsp white wine vinegar
- 1 lime, zested and juiced
- 3 tbsp sunflower oil
- A pinch of sugar
- 1 red chili, deseeded and minced

Instructions:

Add all the slaw ingredients to a bowl except for the peanuts.

In a bowl, mix the dressing ingredients until smooth.

Drizzle half of the dressing on the slaw and mix until well combined.

Add more of the dressing as desired and mix well.

Sprinkle the peanuts on top and serve the coleslaw immediately or chilled.

21. Buttermilk Coleslaw

Adding some buttermilk to standard mayo dressing makes it super creamy and creates a nice buttery flavor to the slaw.

Prep Time: 15 mins

Serves: 4

Ingredients:

Slaw:

- ½ small green cabbage, outer leaves removed and shredded
- 1 large carrot, peeled and shredded
- ½ small red onion, finely shredded

Dressing:

- ½ cup mayonnaise
- 2 tbsp buttermilk
- 1 tsp white vinegar
- ¼ tsp garlic powder
- ½ tsp sugar
- Salt and black to taste

Instructions:

Add all the slaw ingredients to a bowl.

In a bowl, mix the dressing ingredients until smooth.

Drizzle half of the dressing on the slaw and mix until well combined.

Add more of the dressing as desired and mix well.

Serve the coleslaw immediately or chilled.

22. Almond Coleslaw

What a lovely way to use almonds in coleslaw in this straightforward approach that is oh-so-yummy.

Prep Time: 15 mins

Serves: 4

Ingredients:

Slaw:

- 2 cups coleslaw mix
- ½ cup slivered almonds, toasted

Dressing:

- 1 cup mayonnaise
- 2 tbsp cider vinegar
- 1 tbsp sugar
- Salt and black pepper to taste

Instructions:

Add all the coleslaw mix to a bowl.

In a bowl, mix the dressing ingredients until smooth.

Drizzle half of the dressing on the slaw and mix until well combined.

Add more of the dressing as desired and mix well.

Sprinkle the almonds on top and serve the coleslaw immediately or chilled.

23. Pineapple Coleslaw

Some pineapple and broccoli in coleslaw are one to include in your lunch servings. It is super nutritious and surely tastes amazing.

Prep Time: 15 mins

Serves: 4

Ingredients:

Slaw:

- ½ small red cabbage, outer leaves removed and shredded
- 1 cup broccoli slaw mix
- 2 carrots, peeled and shredded
- 1 cup finely chopped fresh pineapple

Dressing:

- ⅓ cup mayonnaise
- 3 tbsp apple cider vinegar
- 2 tbsp fresh lemon juice
- Salt and black pepper to taste

Instructions:

Add all the slaw ingredients to a bowl.

In a bowl, mix the dressing ingredients until smooth.

Drizzle half of the dressing on the slaw and mix until well combined.

Add more of the dressing as desired and mix well.

Serve the coleslaw immediately or chilled.

24. Tahini Coleslaw

This Mediterranean dressed red cabbage coleslaw is one that you will love. Tell us about such elevated flavors.

Prep Time: 15 mins

Serves: 4

Ingredients:

Slaw:

- 1 small red cabbage, shredded
- 3 small carrots, peeled and cut into thin matchsticks
- 1 small onion, thinly shredded

Dressing:

- 5 tbsp Greek yogurt
- 1 ½ tbsp tahini paste
- ½ garlic clove, crushed

Instructions:

Add all the slaw ingredients to a bowl.

In a bowl, mix the dressing ingredients until smooth.

Drizzle half of the dressing on the slaw and mix until well combined.

Add more of the dressing as desired and mix well.

Serve the coleslaw immediately or chilled.

25. Mediterranean Coleslaw

Yet another Mediterranean coleslaw for your timeline that is rich with so many vegetables, herbs, nuts, and a punchy dressing. It is such a pampering serving.

Prep Time: 15 mins

Serves: 4

Ingredients:

Slaw:

- ½ small green cabbage, outer leaves removed and shredded
- ½ small red cabbage, outer leaves removed and shredded
- 1 large carrots, peeled and shredded
- 1 small red bell pepper, deseeded and thinly sliced
- 2 green onions, trimmed and thinly sliced
- 4 large radishes, halved and thinly sliced
- ½ cup chopped fresh dill
- 1 cup chopped parsley
- 1 tsp sumac
- Salt to taste
- 1 cup sliced almonds, toasted

Dressing:

- 2 tbsp Dijon mustard
- ⅓ cup extra-virgin olive oil
- 2 limes, juiced
- 2 garlic cloves, minced
- ½ tsp sumac
- Salt and black pepper to taste

Instructions:

Add all the slaw ingredients to a bowl.

In a bowl, mix the dressing ingredients until smooth.

Drizzle half of the dressing on the slaw and mix until well combined.

Add more of the dressing as desired and mix well.

Serve the coleslaw immediately or chilled.

26. Spicy Avocado Coleslaw

The dressing for this coleslaw is avocado-based and that's where all the magic happens. Have you had an avocado-based coleslaw yet?

Prep Time: 15 mins

Serves: 4

Ingredients:

Slaw:

- ½ small green cabbage, outer leaves removed and shredded
- ½ small red cabbage, outer leaves removed and shredded
- 2 carrots, peeled and shredded
- A handful of fresh parsley, finely chopped

Dressing:

- ½ cup mayonnaise
- 1 avocado, peeled and cut into chunks
- ½ jalapeno pepper, deseeded and minced
- 2 tbsp olive oil
- 2 tbsp apple cider vinegar
- Salt to taste

Instructions:

Add all the slaw ingredients to a bowl.

In a bowl, mix the dressing ingredients until smooth.

Drizzle half of the dressing on the slaw and mix until well combined.

Add more of the dressing as desired and mix well.

Serve the coleslaw immediately or chilled.

27. Beetroot Coleslaw

Try out beetroot for your coleslaw instead of red cabbage and introduce all that rooty flavor into it. We are sure you'll keep making it often.

Prep Time: 15 mins

Serves: 4

Ingredients:

Slaw:

- 1 cup finely shredded beets
- 1 medium carrot, peeled and shredded
- 1 bunch spring onion, thinly sliced
- 1 to 2 tsp toasted cashews

Dressing:

- 3 tbsp plain yogurt
- 1 tsp honey
- A pinch of ginger powder
- A pinch of chili powder

Instructions:

Add all the slaw ingredients to a bowl except for the cashews.

In a bowl, mix the dressing ingredients until smooth.

Drizzle half of the dressing on the slaw and mix until well combined.

Add more of the dressing as desired and mix well.

Sprinkle the cashews on top and serve the coleslaw immediately or chilled.

28. Tahini Turkey Coleslaw

Some tahini and turkey in coleslaw are guaranteed to treat you at dinner so well. Talk of a better way to make coleslaw and this recipe goes deeply in.

Prep Time: 15 mins

Serves: 4

Ingredients:

Slaw:

- ½ small green cabbage, outer leaves removed and shredded
- ½ small red cabbage, outer leaves removed and shredded
- 2 carrots, peeled and cut into thin matchsticks
- 1 red onion, halved and thinly sliced
- 1 green apple, cored julienned
- 1 cup finely chopped cilantro
- ½ cup unsalted toasted peanuts, roughly chopped
- 2 tbsp sesame seeds

Dressing:

- ½ cup plain yogurt
- 5 tbsp tahini paste
- 3 tbsp lime juice
- 1 garlic clove, crushed
- Salt and black pepper to taste

Instructions:

Add all the slaw ingredients to a bowl except for the peanuts.

In a bowl, mix the dressing ingredients until smooth.

Drizzle half of the dressing on the slaw and mix until well combined.

Add more of the dressing as desired and mix well.

Sprinkle the peanuts on top and serve the coleslaw immediately or chilled.

29. Apricot Coleslaw

Some apricot in coleslaw is different but you would surely love the sweetness that each bite offers.

Prep Time: 15 mins

Serves: 4

Ingredients:

Slaw:

- ½ small green cabbage, outer leaves removed and shredded
- 3 small carrots, grated
- ½ red onion, thinly sliced
- ⅓ cup dried apricots, chopped
- ½ cup golden raisins

Dressing:

- 3 tbsp tahini
- 1 tbsp Dijon mustard
- 3 tbsp water
- 2 tsp apple cider vinegar
- 1 tsp maple syrup
- 1 tsp horseradish

Instructions:

Add all the slaw ingredients to a bowl.

In a bowl, mix the dressing ingredients until smooth.

Drizzle half of the dressing on the slaw and mix until well combined.

Add more of the dressing as desired and mix well.

Serve the coleslaw immediately or chilled.

30. Mexican Coleslaw

What is a coleslaw cookbook without a Mexican-styled one? All the elements are right and enriching here. Meanwhile, it does without the mayo but works in some tangy vinaigrette for all that Mexican vibe.

Prep Time: 15 mins

Serves: 4

Ingredients:

Slaw:

- ½ small green cabbage, outer leaves removed and shredded
- ½ small red cabbage, outer leaves removed and shredded
- 2 carrots, peeled and shredded
- ¼ cup chopped fresh cilantro

Dressing:

- ¼ cup lime juice
- 2 tbsp rice vinegar
- ½ tsp cumin powder
- ½ tsp garlic powder
- Salt and black pepper to taste

Instructions:

Add all the slaw ingredients to a bowl.

In a bowl, mix the dressing ingredients until smooth.

Drizzle half of the dressing on the slaw and mix until well combined.

Add more of the dressing as desired and mix well.

Serve the coleslaw immediately or chilled.

Conclusion

Do you have a different perspective about coleslaw now?

We hope these recipes have given you better reasons to make and enjoy coleslaw better.

Coleslaw is a more relaxed way to enjoy salad, so being creative with little elements here and there would elevate it better.

Do enjoy a fun time with it.

Biography

"Cooking is a chore unless you love the process", which is the motto of Tyler Sweet, an extremely talented chef who has made her name in the catering industry with the help of her deep understanding of a variety of ingredients and human taste buds. She had always loved whipping up new recipes as a pass time activity but her career began when she got her first job at a local restaurant and realized that she would not mind doing it forever.

Tyler's hobby blossomed into a passion that drove her up the ladder so quickly that by the end of the year, she was already a sous chef and a rising talent. An impeccable eye for unique mixtures and a willingness to learn new dishes, she has since then worked for over 10 five-star restaurants in the tri-state. Presently, Sweet owns a thriving online cooking class where she has found a great, interactive avenue to teach on her most favorite subject, food.

Author's Note

I really appreciate you taking the time to not just download but also read my book, you don't know but that is the highest compliment you can ever give me. And it may seem greedy but I just have one more favor to ask of you, I need your feedback. Do you have any comments, suggestions, or complaints? Or you have an idea for my next book? Please reach out to me if you like, I'm always available for my loyal readers.

Thank you.

Tyler Sweet

Printed in Great Britain
by Amazon

Louis Harris – Carla Tyler

HOW TO PLAY

HARP

IN EASY WAY

A Complete beginner's Guide illustrated Step by Step.

Features, Easy Instructions, Practice Exercises

to Learn How to Play the Harp

Copyright © 2020 publishing.

All rights reserved.

Author: Louis Harris

No part of this publication may be reproduced, distributed or transmitted in any form or by any means, including photocopying recording or other electronic or mechanical methods or by any information storage and retrieval system without the prior written permission of the publisher, except in the case of brief quotation embodies in critical reviews and certain other non-commercial uses permitted by copyright law.

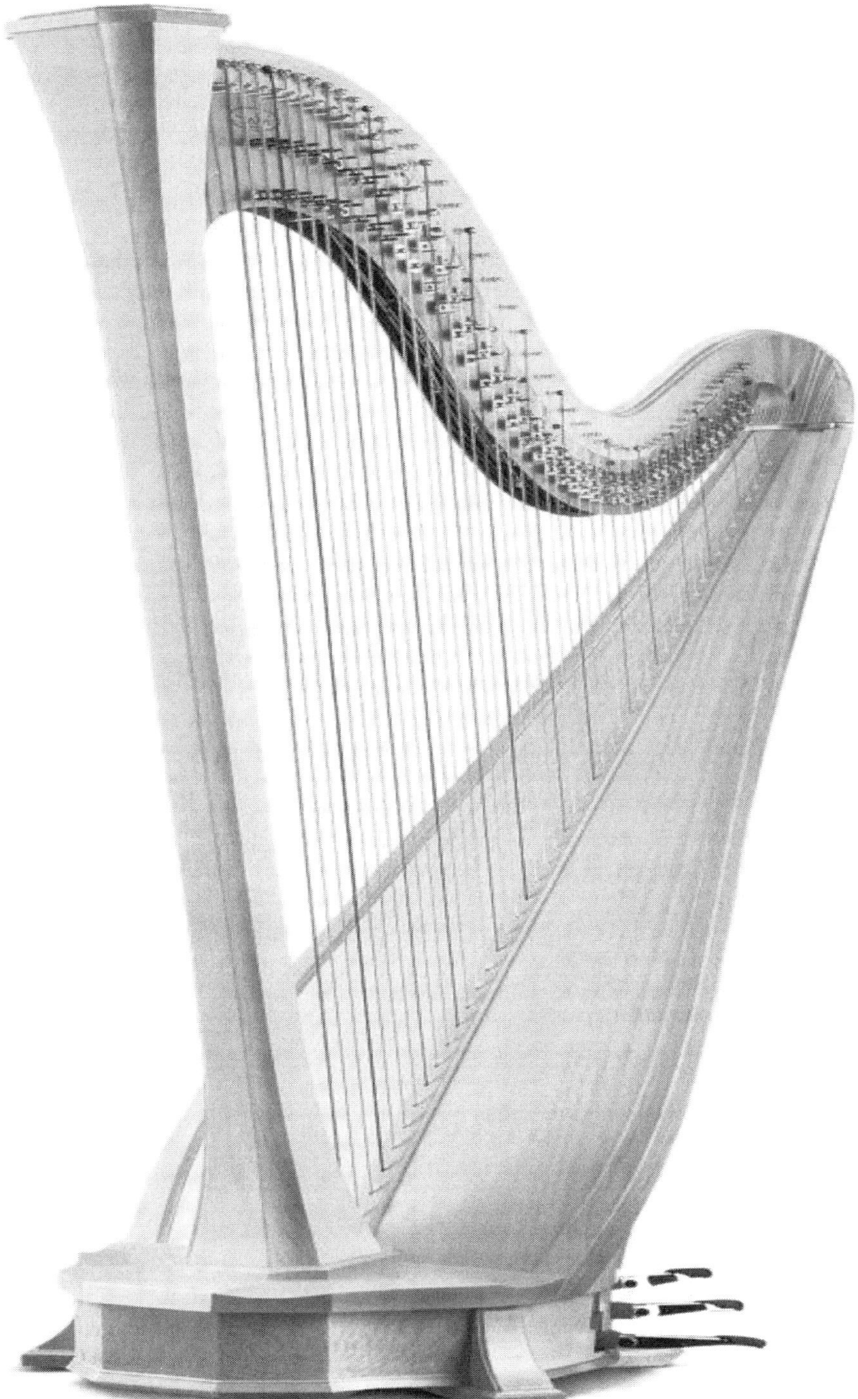

Table Of Contents

History of the Harp

The Irish Harp

Who Should Play the Harp?

The Amount Does a Harp Cost?

Considerations When Buying a Harp

Another Harp Techniques

Learning How to Play Harp

The Blues Harp - Learning to Cross Harp

Tuning a Therapy Harp For Beginners

Ways to Get the Most Out of Your Harp Playing

Using the Harp to Create a Romantic Environment

Practice exercises

History of the Harp

The harp is one of the most established musical instruments on the planet. The soonest harps were created from the chasing bow. The divider artworks of old Egyptian tombs dating from as ahead of schedule as 3000 B.C. show an instrument that intently looks like the tracker's bow, without the column that we find in present-day harps.

The calculated harp came to Egypt from Asia in around 1500 B.C. It was worked from an empty sound-box joined to a straight string-arm at a point. The strings, conceivably made of hair or plant fiber, were connected to the sound-box toward one side and attached to the string-arm at the other. The strings were tuned by pivoting the bunches that held them.

During the Middle Ages, the column was added to help the strain of additional strings. Stiffer string materials like copper and metal were utilized, and these progressions empowered the instrument to create a more prominent volume and a more extended continuing tone. Artistic creations of these harps show up in numerous early compositions, and their shapes barely vary from those of the Celtic harps that are as yet played today.

As the early harps had no mechanical gadgets for giving the player various keys, harpists thought that it was essential to retune those strings they required for each piece. In the long run, in the last 50% of the seventeenth century, a line of metal snares was set along the left half of the harp. At the point when the player physically turned a trap against an individual string, the string's pitch was raised a half advance. Current non-pedal harps are worked with significantly progressed sharping switches introduced for each string, which produces an excellent tonal quality when locked in. Switches are commonly moved with the left hand, and gifted players can accomplish changes rapidly.

The most accurate known delineation of an edge harp in the British Isles is on an eighth-century stone cross. Music was a significant piece of life in antiquated Ireland, and the harp was a noble instrument, played in the courts of rulers and before the head of tribes. Harpers were required to have the option to summon three unique feelings in their crowd by their music: Laughter, tears, and rest.

With the Anglicisation of the Irish respectability, the conventional harpers became minstrels and road musicians discussing verse and singing society melodies to the backup of their harps.

At some point before 1720, a system created to fulfill the developing needs from harpists for an instrument that was fit for a more extensive scope of the pitch. Seven pedals incorporated with the base of the harp could raise the ball considerably a stage. For example, on the off chance that the harp was tuned to C-level, at that point, discouraging the pedal would raise the C strings to C-characteristic. The single activity harp conceived.

The single activity harp accomplished extraordinary notoriety all through the remainder of the eighteenth century, as was proved in the French Court by Marie Antoinette; maybe, the most celebrated player of this instrument. The harps of this period eminently embellished with help cutting, sumptuously plated, and hand-painted. Other than being musical instruments, they were without a doubt prized as article d'art when shown in the plated salons of the period.

As music developed, it was additionally important for the harp, if it somehow happened to keep up its fame, to move with the occasions. Rather than just being restricted to eight important keys and five minor keys, it had gotten indispensable significant for the harp to have the option to played in all keys. Because of this need, Sebastian Erard got a patent in 1810 for the Double Action pedal harp.

Erard overhauled the single activity instrument, supplanting the stitches with two pivoting pronged plates. The strings, presently each outfitted with two plates, had the option to create a level, healthy and a sharp relying upon the situation of the relating pedal, permitting the harpist to play in each key.

This crafty creation altered the harp is still being used today. The harp has since kept on developing and has had numerous noteworthy enhancements made to the course of the recent hundreds of years. In the late 1800's Lyon and Healy, a Chicago based organization that is as yet constructing harps today started fabricating harps in America with incredibly reinforced edges and numerous significant enhancements to Erard's twofold activity instrument.

Because of the proceeded with the prevalence of the harp into the twentieth century, numerous other harp producers landed on the scene, each bringing their upgrades and developments without which the instrument would not have had the option to keep up its a dependable balance in current society. In America, other than Lyon and Healy, some other pedal harp producers incorporate Wurlitzer, Venus, and Swanson. Some extra producers in Europe incorporate Salvi, Camac, Horngacher, David, and Thurau, just as Aoyama in Japan.

The 21st century holds incredible guarantee for the proceeded with a prominence of the harp as is proved by the horde celebrations, shows, social orders, harp builders, music, exhibitions, and profession openings accessible to harpists.

From Medieval to Modern, from Classical to Jazz, from Acoustic to Electric. The harp is an instrument saturated with convention yet open to change, and for some, it is more than an insignificant instrument; it is a calling.

The Irish Harp

The harp that once through Tara's lobbies the spirit of music shed, presently hangs as quiet on Tara's dividers, as though that spirit was fled.

So, dozes the pride of previous days, so greatness' rush is o'er, what's more, hearts that once beat high for acclaim, presently feel that heartbeat no more

To tell the historical backdrop of the Irish harp is to tell the historical backdrop of the Irish individuals. This antiquated people instrument with its wonderful, sensitive sound is played today in spite of being disregarded, scorned and restricted for a considerable length of time. Harpers, who in prior days would have been hanged for their specialty, presently thrive all through the world, as do the Irish themselves

Legend reveal to us the main harp was possessed by Dagda, a boss among the Tuatha De Danaan. At once during a war with the Fomorians, the divine forces of cold and murkiness, his harp was taken yet later recuperated by Lugh and Ogma. At the point when it was returned it had gained two mystery names and the capacity to call forward summer and winter. From that point on, when Dagda played, he could create a tune so powerful, it would cause his crowd to sob, he could play an air so glad it would make everybody grin, or deliver a sound so peaceful, it would calm all who tuned in to rest. So in this way did the harp turned into the distributor of Sorrow, Gladness and Rest.

Harps are played all through a significant part of the world. From old works of art, epic stories and verse, we learn of harps in Babylonia and Mesopotamia. We see them in the tomb of Pharaoh Ramses III , votive carvings from Iraq and figures of antiquated Greece. From Africa, which has in excess of 100 harp customs, the instrument headed out north to Spain and before long spread all through Europe. Hung with ligament, silk or wire, harps shift in size, structure and adornment as indicated by the physical and innovative conditions of their inceptions. African harps have been produced using wood and gourd secured with cowhide, the Burmese sang auk has an angled soundbox like the Turkish ceng while European harps highlight a triangular edge, There is one component that all harps share: the strings run vertical (as opposed to resemble) to the sound box.

Griffith of Wales utilized harpists in his court toward the finish of the eleventh century and the priest history specialist Geraldus Cambrensis appreciated the incredible expertise of the Irish harpers and commented that some even believed the Scots to be better players. For Irish and Scottish harpers regularly visited each other's nations to consider, to learn and trade tunes and their music was appreciated all through Europe. Another twelfth century documenter, John of Salisbury, composed that " ... had it not been for the Irish harp, there would have been no music at all on the Crusades."

These harps were very unique in relation to the huge pedal harps we find in present day ensemble symphonies. They were a lot littler, initially hung on the harper's lap, inclining toward the left shoulder, had no pedals, and typically were cut in one piece from swamp wood. The Trinity College Harp and Queen Mary's Harp are the most established enduring Celtic harps and both date from the fifteenth or sixteenth hundreds of years and represent the likeness between the Irish and Scottish harps. A distinctive trait of these Gaelic harps was that they were wire-hung, instead of gut hung. "Harp" has its foundations in the Anglo-Saxon, Old German and Old Norse words which signify "to cull." In Gaelic they were referred to first as cruit and later as clarsach or cláirseach.

The harp isn't particular to Ireland yet in this manner turned into its national image. (These days you can even observe it on the Guinness mark) Harpers were profoundly prepared experts who performed for the respectability and appreciated political force - to such an extent that during the sixteenth century, Queen Elizabeth I gave an announcement to hang Irish harpists and devastate their instruments to forestall insurgence.

Unfortunately, while this most seasoned image of Ireland is still with us today the vast majority of the antiquated pretense and songs it once created are a distant memory, however more youthful harpers are responding to the call to stir the pride of previous days.

Who Should Play the Harp?

Anybody that needs to should take up the harp. The harp is most importantly an instrument of the individuals. From extravagant symphonies to medieval Celtic laborers, the harp has a long history of fitting anybody with the inspiration to rehearse it. Little treatment harps are even intended for individuals who are out of commission. If you want to seek after a harp, you should attempt it. There are more reasonable harps available than there were before. There are rental plans accessible that are currently less expensive than a telephone bill!

The Amount Does a Harp Cost?

Before all else, you may get overpowered with how costly a harp can be. It's a smart thought to make sense of the amount you can spend on your first harp, and consider.

You know best your own spending limit and how genuine a harp you need to take on-organizations like Salvi, Teifi and Morley harps have "beginners" or "understudy" harps that start at around £1500-£2000.

At the opposite finish of the scale, you can purchase a Pakistani-made harp for around £400. These do have somewhat of a ropey notoriety, so do your examination and purchaser be careful (don't simply trust me, I am, all things considered, rivaling them).

We make a harp in the UK, the Morwenna Rose 27 string, for £650 (without levers). This harp was structured considering beginners, being sufficiently light to take to exercises/society club with a sound that stands facing significantly more costly challenge.

Levers

Another thought, identified with cost, is whether to have a harp with levers on.

The difficulty is that tolerable levers cost fair cash. You can get modest levers; however, they frequently don't function admirably they can buzz and regularly don't raise the string by precisely a half tone-fundamentally the harp will sound off key. Better than average levers are costly and getting an unlevered harp may be a decent choice.

Levers present the complexities of key changes, and aren't generally fundamental for the main year or so when the most significant thing is to grow acceptable propensities and train your fingers to play various examples.

You can't hit a note that sounds awful on an unlevered harp since every one of the strings will be in the correct key!

Orchestral Pedal Harp

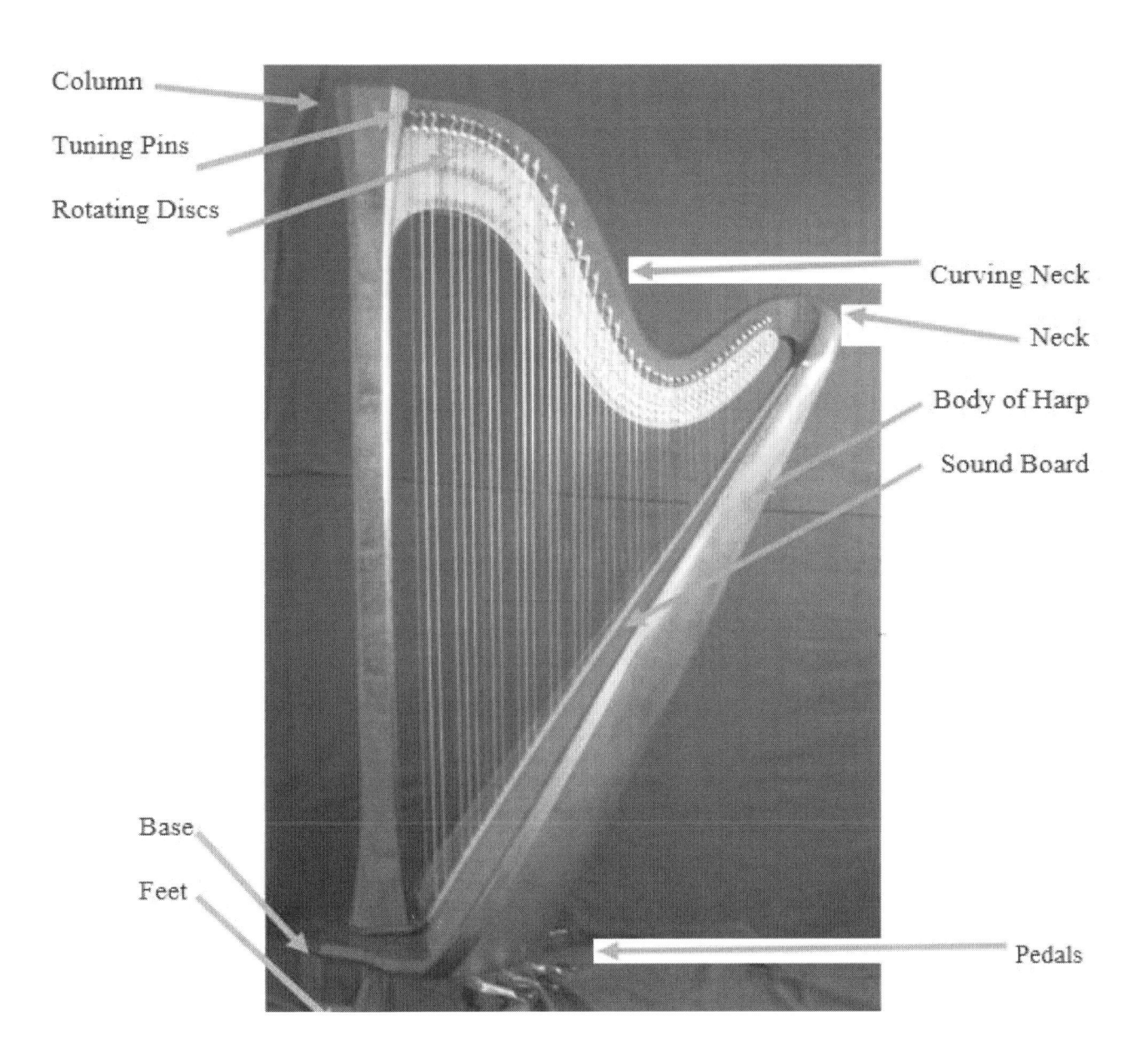

- Column
- Tuning Pins
- Rotating Discs
- Curving Neck
- Neck
- Body of Harp
- Sound Board
- Base
- Feet
- Pedals

What number of strings?

An inquiry I get posed to a great deal is, "What number of strings does a harp have?" It's hard not to be wry with my answer and answer with "to what extent is a bit of harp string?". You can get a "harp" with as not many as ten strings. However, it's mostly a toy. Harps additionally accompany as not many as 22 or even 19 strings. However, there's very little you can play on them.

We make a 27 string harp necessarily because that is a harp with a better than average range-there is a lot of music that you can play on a 27 string harp. You can get harps with 44 or even 48 strings, and more than that when you think about triple hung harps! However, these expenses as much as another vehicle.

Another thought would be whether you need to experience the ABRSM and Trinity reviews on your first harp.

The vast majority would presumably update before they finish their evaluation tests, and you need in any event 34 strings on a completely turned harp to arrive at grade 8. Numerous harpers don't experience the evaluations by any means.

This depends whether you have your sights on society clubs and open-air fires or than show corridors and ensembles. Or, on the other hand, to put it another way, do you seek to be harper or a harpist?

What are the arms reach of the new artist? Commonly kids and individuals with physical trouble can't stretch around the enormous body of a 34 string harp or a pedal harp.

Anything 34 string and bigger is likewise going to be overwhelming, so whether you can oversee conveying that weight is an interesting point. Not all vehicles can even fit 34 string harps, not to mention a pedal harp.

Considerations When Buying a Harp

A harp is a superb instrument. On the off chance that you are hoping to buy another or utilized harp there are a few qualities of the harp to take a gander at. These things incorporate the size, development, and the tone.

Is anything but a smart thought to purchase a harp online except if you know the specific size of the harp you need to purchase. It is generally best to go to a neighborhood instrument shop and sit with a harp in position to be certain it fits you right. If you are purchasing a harp for a kid it is critical to be certain the kid can arrive at the pedals easily. It is normally best to purchase a littler harp that gauges short of what it is to buy a greater one that can cause hurt if the player doesn't have the solidarity to control it or hold it in position.

The best harp for amateurs is the floor harp that has 27 to 30 strings. The semi fantastic harps are best for more seasoned players since it is littler in tallness and doesn't gauge a great deal. This harp has 46 strings. The show fantastic harp is utilized for the most part by the expert musicians and they have 47 strings.

It is significant when you are purchasing a harp to tune in to the tone of the harp. On the off chance that you are a learner and you don't have the foggiest idea what to tune in for it is critical to carry somebody with you who is experienced and recognizes what to tune in for. You may have a music exercise instructor who can assist you with the choice.

The tone ought to be brilliant, warm and venture well indeed. Be that as it may, you don't need a lot of both characteristics or the sound may not sound well by any means.

The development of a harp ought to be well-made to guarantee the life span. Furthermore, a very much made harp will keep up the worth since it utilizes wood of good quality, sounds astonishing, and has an amazing pressure on the strings. Make certain to check if the pedals are not twisted, the completion is smooth and there is no harm in the wood, the neck isn't distorted, and the sections are straight, and there are no holes in the sound box. Also, the base should be solidly joined to the feet of the harp.

Purchasing a harp is a major choice since they can be over the top expensive.

There are numerous things to take a gander at to decide you are getting a quality instrument. It is a smart thought to have somebody go with you to choose a harp if you are new to the instrument.

Another Harp Techniques

Lever Harp

For this starting harp technique book, the switch harp can be tuned in the key of C Major. All notes, with their levers in the down position, will enlist as naturals on a chromatic tuner.

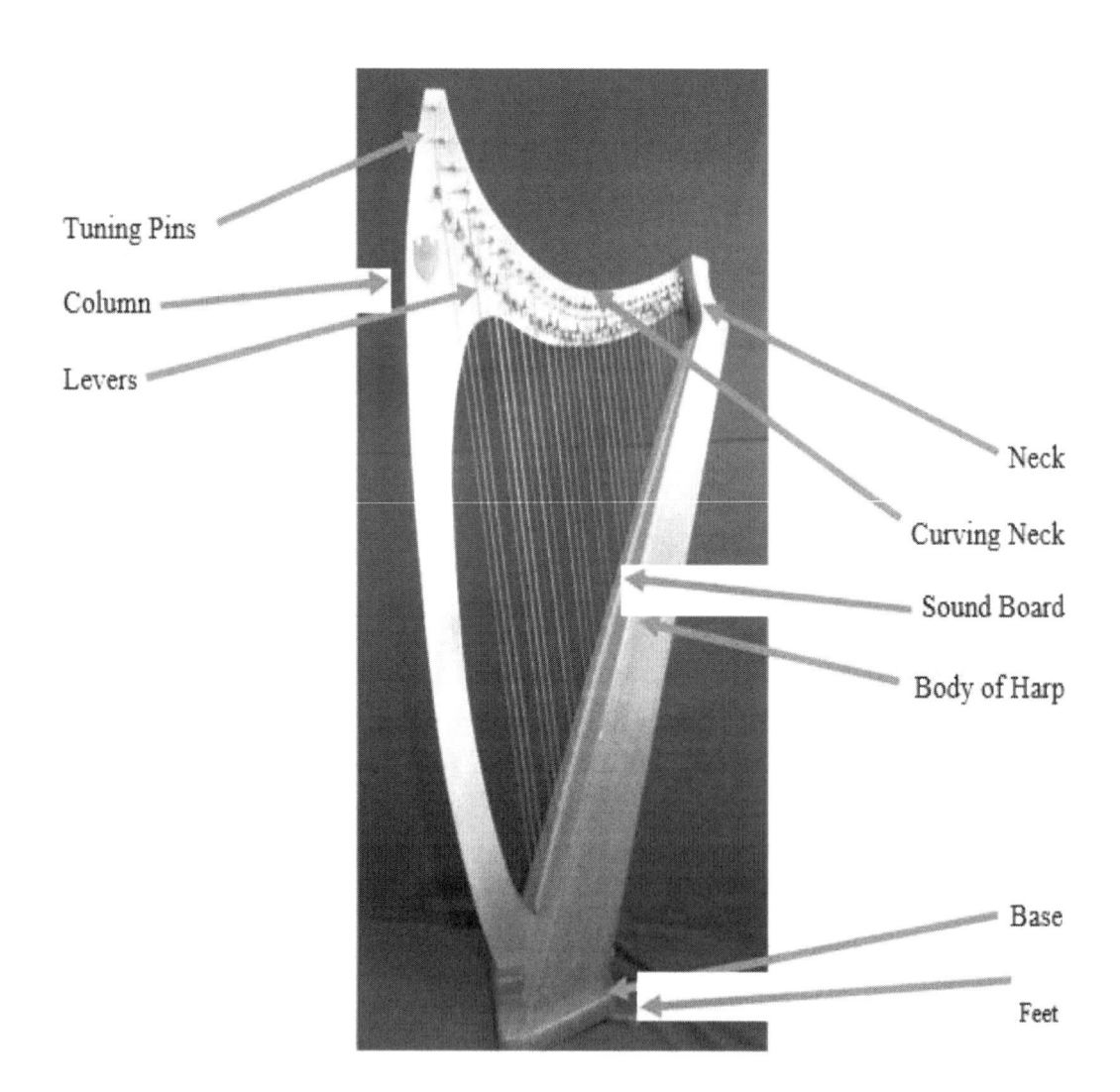

- Tuning Pins
- Column
- Levers
- Neck
- Curving Neck
- Sound Board
- Body of Harp
- Base
- Feet

Pedal Harp

Pedals harps ought to consistently be tuned in the key of C-level Major. All pedals ought to be in their level position or the first class. A decent method to check is to check whether there is any component contacting the highest point of the string. Nothing ought to be approaching the most upper end of the string.

BOTH

Just utilize a harp tuning key on the tuning pegs. When not turning a peg, remove the tuning key from the harp; many tuning keys are shrouded inelastic, yet if they fall them despite everything that could harm the harp. To fix the string and make it keener, turn the tuning key toward the front of the harp, away from you. To disengage the string and lower the pitch, turn the tuning key toward the little piece of the harp, or you.

Technique 1

Start at center C (center red string), tune each string stepwise down the harp (close to the first post). At that point, come back to the center of the harp and tune stepwise up toward the top. It is turning a pedal harp, and you will have the entirety of the pedals in their level position and tuning in CB.

Technique 2

Start at center C, and then tune every C all over the harp. Proceed up the scale tuning all the D strings, at that point all the E strings, and so on.

Technique 3

Tune in interims of fourths and fifths. One can follow this technique in two different ways: the main, every octave independent from anyone else, and the second two by two notes. The primary, tune center C, at that point, the G above, at that point the D underneath and the an above. Follow the example of up a fifth, down a fourth, up a fifth. The following way, tune the entirety of your Cs and Gs; at that point, the whole of the Ds and As, Es and Bs, and then end with Fs and Cs.

For Each Technique

Tune the harp each day. Each harmonica is extraordinary. You will discover a technique that functions admirably for you as you find a pleasant pace harp you are working with. Likewise, as you find a pleasant pace harp, you will locate that a few octaves leave tune more often than others and maybe balanced while you are playing.

Care of Instrument

1. Continuously handle your instrument with care. Be mindful so as not to knock the wood with anything around the instrument, for example, your seat or music stand, as it might make the instrument leave tune and need altering.

2. Tune your instrument day by day. In addition to the fact that it is smarter to build up your ear as an artist by hearing an instrument that is in order, however it is better for the instrument to hold the planned pressure of the strings. For help on tuning, see Appendix B.

3. Never leave the tuning key on the tuning pegs as it might fall and could harm the instrument.

4. Continuously spread your instrument when you are not utilizing it.

5.The harp ought to never be in outrageous hot or cold temperatures. It is ideal, if conceivable, to keep the harp along an inside divider in a room that will keep a consistent temperature between about 65°F and 75°F.

6. Do not attempt your repairs. Only a trained harp technician should handle repairing your harp.

7. Always wash your hands before handling your instrument.

8. Do not let others play your instrument.

Fundamental Considerations

1. Fingernails should always be kept short.

2. Clothing should always cover your knees when playing your instrument. Oils and dirt from your skin can damage the wood.

3. The red strings are noted the name "C," and the black or blue strings are noted name "F."

Accessories

1. Tuning key

2. Chromatic Tuner

3. Seat or bench of the correct height

4. Soft cloth

5. Music stand

6. Music folder

7. Metronome

Instrument Position

1. Sit in the middle of the chair or stool, neither too close to the edge nor to the back.

   a. Sit erect, without slouching or being too tense.
   b. Please pay attention to your shoulders as you play; they should not rise.

Left: *Sitting correctly at a pedal harp with the instrument on the floor*

Right: *Sitting correctly at a lever harp with the instrument on the floor*

2.The right tallness of the seat or stool is dictated by where the harpist's hands lay on the strings. If the hands are excessively high on the strings, the seat is excessively high. If the hands are excessively low on the strings, the seat is excessively low. The hands ought to be put easily at the center of the strings.

3.The instrument ought to be put exceptionally straight before the correct shoulder, with the goal that when pulled back it lays on the correct shoulder just as within the two knees.

4. When not on pedals, the two feet ought to be level on the floor, not crossed or tucked under the seat.

Hand Position while Playing Harp

Left: H and position for the right hand.

Right: Hand position for the left hand.

1. Hands ought to be bended, keeping up an empty in the palm a s if holding a tennis ball.

2. Fingers ought to be marginally inclined descending. Just four badgers are utilized. The fifth (pinky) is too short and excessively powerless. The fifth finger ought to rather follow the fourth (ring finger).

3. Knuckles ought to be bended marginally out and the strings plucked with simply fingertips.

4.Wrists ought to be in a characteristic situation, as they are while resting the whole lower arm on a table.

5. Forearms are commonly corresponding to the floor.

6.Thumbs should be raised higher than the remainder of the fingers, making a bend between the thumb and second (pointer) and making an empty in the palm.

7.Both hands should be nearly a similar level on the strings, with the left somewhat lower than the right.

8. After playing, the hand should close totally, freely, with the fingers level and not bended under.

Learning How to Play Harp

- Tune your harp. New harps should be tuned, and you should tune your harp each couple of times that you play it. You can cautiously fix or relax the strings to change the notes by utilizing the tuning key that accompanied the harp. This is a region where an accomplished artist will be of incredible assistance to you. On the off chance that you have not gained a solid ear for music, you can utilize an electric tuner.

- On the off chance that you have a pedal harp, be certain that all pedals are withdrawn before tuning. Spot each pedal in the level key, which is the first class.

- On the off chance that you have a switch harp, be certain all levers are withdrawn. With your switch harp, you will most likely first tune to the key of C Major.

- Investigate the strings. They resemble the keys on a piano: A,B,C,D,E,F,G rehashed again and again.

The red strings are Cs, the dark or blue strings are Fs. On the off chance that you would already be able to play the piano, the strings will come all the more normally to you, and you will no doubt become acclimated to the strings a lot quicker than non-piano players.

- Play the harp with your thumb and initial three fingers. Most harps are played with the delicate sides or tips of your thumb and initial three fingers. When playing a switch or pedal harp, fingernails must be kept short except if you need a brazen sound. Wire-hung harps and certain propelled procedures for different harps are played with the fingernails.

- Play around with the strings. You don't have to know the entirety of the notes or even ability to peruse music to create a delightful sound on a harp. Utilizing what you know up until this point, utilize your fingers to tenderly cull the strings. Play around until you feel great with utilizing the harp.

- You should become familiar with the notes and read music sooner or later in the event that you are not kidding about the harp, yet don't stress over that an excessive amount of when you are a beginner.

- Attempt a fundamental glissando. Hold out the thumb of your playing hand. Spot it on the harp strings the extent that you can reach. Push it rapidly away from you in a descending movement with the goal that it slides and makes each string ring out. At that point, pull it rapidly towards you in an upward movement.
- Be mindful so as not to let your knuckles breakdown as you do this, as that will diminish the sound quality.

- Endeavor an essential tune. A basic tune you can attempt to play is "Column Row Your Boat." First, pluck the "C" string. After you've culled it, close your fingers into your palm, shaping a light clench hand. You will do this after each note you pluck. To play this melody, pluck these notes:

C CDE EDEFG

C GGG EEE CCC

GFE DC

The Blues Harp - Learning to Cross Harp

A diatonic instrument is intended to play in just a single musical key. You need an alternate one for each unique musical key that you need to play in. An instrument that can play in any key is a chromatic instrument. The diatonic harmonica was first mass created by Matthias Hohner in 1857. By 1858 he started transporting them to America. They were intended to play German and European society music. They adjusted well to American people and Country music. The harmonica that I figured out how to play on was the Hohner Marine Band. It was the fundamental diatonic ten opening harmonica which has been sold in that structure from 1920.

The essential diatonic ten opening harmonica is intended to play basic significant key tunes. The agreement of these tunes depends on the tonic major and predominant seventh harmony of a significant scale. As these are based on the first and fifth note of the significant scale they are frequently related to roman numerals as the I and V7 harmonies. Blues congruity is unique. It's two primary harmonies depend on the first and fourth note of the significant scale. In roman numerals that would be an I and IV harmony.

Additionally, both these harmonies could be prevailing sevenths. Lets, utilize the C significant scale to help clarify.

The common music tones are a, b, c, d, e, f, and g. On the off chance that you start on the note c, you have c, d, e, f, g, a, b, c. this gives you the do, re, me, fa, along these lines, la, ti, do of a significant scale. Start on some other note and you need sharps or pads to make it a significant scale contingent upon which note you start on. In the key of C major The I and V7 harmonies are C and G7. Assume we need to play blues in the key of G major. The significant scale notes are g, a, b, c, d, e, f sharp, g. The I and IV harmonies would be G or G7 and C or C7 for blues. The fifth note of the C scale is G and four up from that is C. So you can see that in the event that we take the harmonies for a basic tune in the key of C major and play them in reverse, utilizing the V harmony for the I and the I for the IV, we have blues in G major.

Presently we have to know the notes in the harmonies. For some harmonies, we take the note we start with and afterward every other note. The recipe is 1, 3, 5 for a significant harmony. So for a C significant harmony beginning on c, the notes are c, e, g. At the point when you blow into the ten opening diatonic harmonica in the key of C major, the notes are c, e, g, c, e, g, c, e, g, c. At the end of the day when you are blowing into the harmonica, you are playing a C significant harmony. Beginning a g for a g7 harmony we have 1, 3, 5, 7. So the notes in the G7 harmony are g, b, d, f.. At the point when you breath in or draw on the ten gap diatonic harmonica in the key of C major, the notes are d, g, b, d, f, a, b, d, f, a. The note an isn't one of the essential notes of the G7 harmony however it works out positively for it. So when you are drawing on the harmonica, you are essentially playing a G 7 harmony.

At the point when you play the diatonic harmonica the manner in which it was intended to be played, you figure out how to play the tune notes as you cover and reveal different openings with your tongue. With you tongue prevailing over a harmony backup to the song and your measured hands making different impacts, you really solid like a little band. How did this basic people instrument become a blues harp. In the 1920's harmonica players started to find how to get an alternate sound. They found that in the event that you played it in reverse, utilizing the draw harmony as your essential harmony and the blow harmony as your auxiliary harmony, you got a blues sound. It's called cross harping. With your harmonies being G7 on the draw and C on the blow, you are playing blues in G on your C harmonica. This is called cross harping. Include the strategy of over attracting to twist the notes and intensification and you're feeling down harp. At the point when you hear it performed by a practiced player, it's astounding the sounds that they escape such a basic instrument.

The diatonic harmonica is the principal instrument that I figured out how to play. The principal melody I figured out how to play was "Gracious Susanna". I didn't figure out how to play it as a blues instrument until numerous years after the fact. I have a great deal of free music exercises on my site however not on playing the harmonica. Since I've composed this article, I'm going to put one there. Until I do there are loads of free exercises on music and playing piano and guitar.

Tuning a Therapy Harp For Beginners

Getting your first harp is an extraordinary encounter. The stuff of fantasies and legends that turns into a piece of your existence. Since forever harps have been a piece of the human experience. From Bards and Minstrels playing to engage those devouring in the eating corridor to War harps being determined to the highest point of slopes sending unnerving sounds downward on the foe in a fight. How you tune your harp relies upon what sort of music you hope to play.

These guidelines are especially for Celtic or Therapy Harps with simply the strings (no switches). You may have heard that a few people tune their musical instruments by ear. This capacity requires intense and exact hearing. This is combined with a skillful comprehension of the sound of musical notes. For all of us an instrument tuner is a fundamental bit of hardware.

Pick a battery worked tuner. Any place you go with your instrument your tuner ought to have the option to fit effectively into the pocket of your instrument convey sack or case. Make sure to put your name on the tuner. Check the tuning of your instrument before each playing session. On the off chance that you have another harp it can take half a month for the strings to hold their notes reliably.

Start by putting the tuning key on the tuning peg for Middle C. Center C is the red hued string in the harp. From Middle C tune each string thusly doing the more extended strings with more profound notes first. The return to Middle C and tune the shorter strings. Every red string is a C note and each blue string is a F note.

The length of the string one octave higher than Middle C is a large portion of the length of the Middle C string. The C note string one octave lower than Middle C is double the length of the Middle C string.

At the point when you must supplant a messed up or frayed string. Requesting the right length of string is significant.

In any case the string you request may not be sufficiently long. Likewise note that various octaves may utilize strings of various thicknesses. Educate the string provider which string you are supplanting.

On the off chance that this is the first occasion when you have tuned a harp, at that point locate a peaceful spot where no other sound is rivaling the notes of the harp.

Hold the tuner as near the strings as workable for clear solid acknowledgment. Change the tuning peg with extremely little 1/eighth or 1/4 turns. Unwind and appreciate the experience. It might take more than one session to tune every one of the strings.

Ways to Get the Most Out of Your Harp Playing

1. Practice with each hand isolated. Practice a measure at a time right hand alone at that point disregarded hand at that point set up together, at that point move to the following measure. So as to oppose the impulse to play the entire piece through – go through clingy notes to cover the measures encompassing the one you are learning.

2. Get familiar with the piece back-ward. Rather than continually beginning at the main note and faltering all the way to the finish, gain proficiency with the last expression, at that point the alongside last state heading off to the end, above and beyond back setting off to the end. When you find a good pace express, you have the rest learned. On the off chance that you can't make sense of the expressions, take a gander at gatherings of 4 or 8 measures. Frequently those are your expressions.

3. As a matter of fact Practice! Depression your body, brain, and fingers multiple times 10 minutes per day. ANY measure of training is superior to none by any stretch of the imagination. Keep in mind, your body, psyche, and fingers are muscles that need to assimilate and get familiar with the data in (practice) just as rest from that data. A long distance race practice session, regardless of whether it's just 1 hour for you, isn't generally the best. Attempt to get at your instrument multiple times 10 minutes per day. You may be shocked at the amount you're learning. And appreciate DOING it. Thought from the Blue Cross Blue Shield of Minnesota... a la harp

4. Control the Tempo. Practice gradually and step by step develop speed.

5. Start Small. Practice little areas one after another, with heaps of redundancy. In some cases this implies just 2 or 3 beats one after another, and once in a while a couple of lines.

6. Learning Rhythms. Experiencing difficulty with a cadence? Sing it, at that point step or move the musicality. Getting the cadence into your body will make it playable on the harp.

7. Don't simply play through your music. Avoid the simple parts; they're simple! Locate the hard parts, slow them down, and practice them until you can play them directly at the correct beat.

(tips 8-11 were taken from Dr. Tom Gibson)

8. Unwind. In this day and age, it is unimaginably hard to have a "tranquil personality". A peaceful personality is sans one of interruptions and can concentrate on a solitary issue. With the attack of data and/or tactile pictures besieging us regularly, no big surprise we think that its difficult to accomplish a tranquil personality. All things considered, it is urgent that we do as such. Locate a peaceful room in which to rehearse. At that point, before lay your hands on your harp, take one moment or two to CALM DOWN. A couple of extremely profound, truly moderate breaths does ponders for both the body and the psyche.

9. Have a Plan. At whatever point and any place you're playing, have an objective at the top of the priority list. Let yourself know: "Today I'm going to play each expression with intriguing elements." Or, "Right now, focusing on a smooth legato." Or, "This month I'm going to concentrate on my strategy… "

As should be obvious, you should set long haul AND momentary objectives. You may have objectives for the afternoon, month or year. Or on the other hand, you may have objectives for ONE NOTE!

10. Have a Pencil. In your training zone… at practice… at exercises… have a pencil at hand! Truly, I know we as a whole have shocking recollections, however a pencil always remembers. An error, for example, an off-base note or off base dynamic is excusable ONCE! Imprint it and it won't occur once more.

Other than these conspicuous errors, a pencil can help you to remember substitute positions, accidentals, or certain emphases in a given expression. To put it plainly, the pencil IS your memory! Numerous incredible players have built up their own "shorthand" of images and markings they use to help them in execution.

11. Musical Lines. Regardless of what lies before us on the stand, we ought to consistently regard it as MUSIC. This goes for warm-ups, scales, pieces, concertos, totally everything that you play. Try not to permit your cerebrum to go on "auto-pilot" when heating up; attempt to make expressive and significant musical lines from the most ordinary material. This can be exceptionally testing when dealing with scales! Be that as it may, recollect, 99.9% of the music you'll play depends on scales.

A few deceives that to utilize are dynamic variety, enunciation variety, musical variety, and mental symbolism. By mental symbolism, I mean envisioning yourself in various conditions when playing your scales. You may imagine that you're trying out for the New York Philharmonic and your entire tryout relies on the musical exactness of this ONE scale! Or on the other hand, imagine that your showing a masterclass and exhibiting legitimate finger strategy! (You will be astonished at how centered you can become around a something else "exhausting" scale.)

When dealing with "genuine music", at that point, you are as of now inclined to making musical lines. (We're animals of propensity, recollect?).

Attempt to decide the writer's perspective and consequently his/her INTENT recorded as a hard copy the music before you. Come at the situation from their perspective and hear through their ears. Are there unpretentious subtleties in the music that you're absent?

Is the strength composed increasingly like an electric guitar specialty or is it progressively quelled? Would this be able to state be played in a rubato style or would it be a good idea for me to play it in exacting time?

Am I the most significant voice now or would it be advisable for me to play under the clarinet? Do these staccato markings infer a short, "pecky" style or ought to there be more "meat" on these notes?

These contemplations are what make MUSIC out of a mishmash of dark dabs. These kinds of inquiries are truly unlimited in scope and extremely abstract. Your translation might be totally legitimate, while another person may see it or hear it in a very different light.

This is the innate magnificence of music... abstract understanding and execution. a.k.a. SELF-EXPRESSION! Continuously stay open to new conceivable outcomes and consistently have a purpose behind playing the way you do. (as such, connect with your mind!!!).

Not many undertakings will permit you the scope for self-articulation and innovativeness that is managed you in music.

Using the Harp to Create a Romantic Environment

The harp is a musical instrument that makes an unwinding and extraordinary sound that to many typifies serenity and a feeling of harmony. In the event that you are seeing approaches to make a sentimental situation in your way of life, deciding to actualize a harp is an extraordinary method to carry sentiments of exotic nature to your environment.

Probably the most mainstream sorts of music to play on a harp are old style, celtic just as sacrosanct music from an assortment of kinds.

A harp isn't a simple musical instrument to play and it can take a very long time for an individual to accomplish flawlessness when playing the harp. On the off chance that you need to have harp music played at your next sentimental recess, you should enlist a harpist.

Here are a couple of proposals with respect to where you may use the guide of a streaming harp to bring delicate, erotic music to the ears of people around you.

Weddings-Playing a harp at your wedding makes a definitive sentimental gathering. You can have the harp playing while visitors are trusting that the lady of the hour will stroll down the passageway. You can likewise have the harp playing unobtrusively during the service just as a while later.

Sentimental Dinner with Your Significant Other

Make a feeling of climate as you and your accomplice set up for a night of serene music played by a harpist while you eat. Your feeling of pressure will reduce and the progression of the night will lead towards delicate discussions that will bring you two closer together.

Spoiling Your Loved One

Need to spoil your accomplice this evening? Have a spa or an air pocket shower set up as a shock? Make the event one stride further by having some sentimental harp music playing out of sight. You can undoubtedly accomplish this by setting a CD into your stereo that has the quiet stable of the harp playing out of sight. Harp music will permit the spoiled individual to slip into profound unwinding.

Commemoration Party for the Happy Couple

If you are arranging a commemoration party for a couple whether it be for yourself or your folks, discovering some smooth heart meaning music is an incredible setting to any commemoration repel. Have the harpist at the portal of the gathering to invite visitors and set the state of mind for the night. The environment will keep quiet and unobtrusive for the whole night.

Regardless of what the occasion; the flexibility of the harp can be utilized for any event you need to depict a feeling of exotic nature in your environment.

Practice Exercises

Traditional Hymm

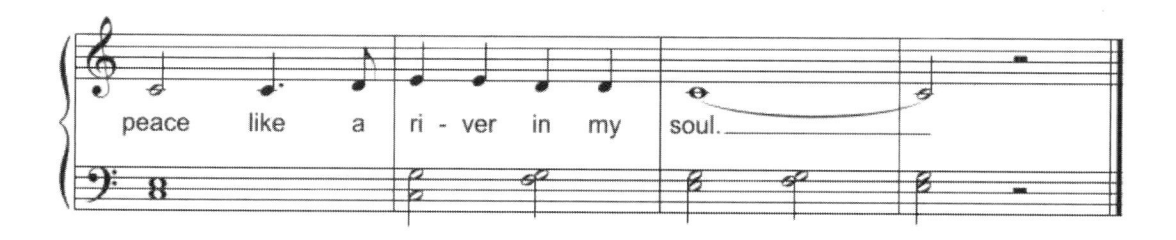

Jesus loves Me

Andante

Harp

mp

Je - sus loves me, this, I know, For the Bi - ble tells me so;

Lit - tle ones to Him be - long, they are weak, but He is strong.

Yes, Je - sus loves me, Yes, Je - sus loves me,

Yes, Je - sus loves me, The Bi - ble tells me so.

Scottish patriotic Song

Jingle Bells

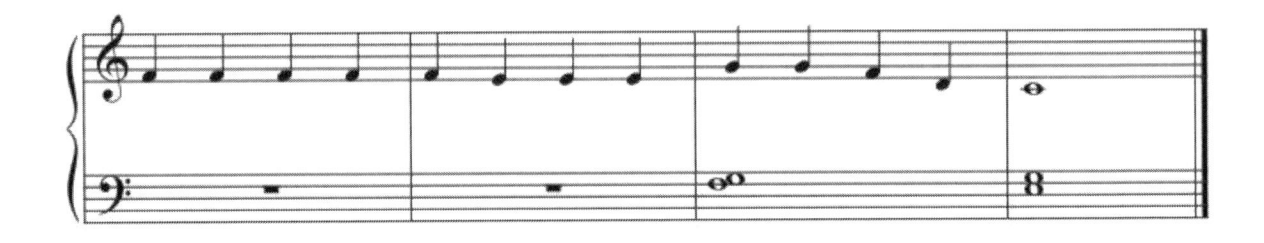

Books by the same author:

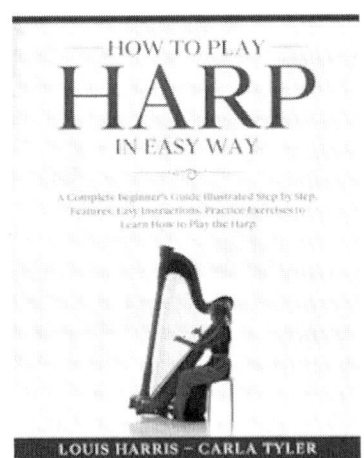

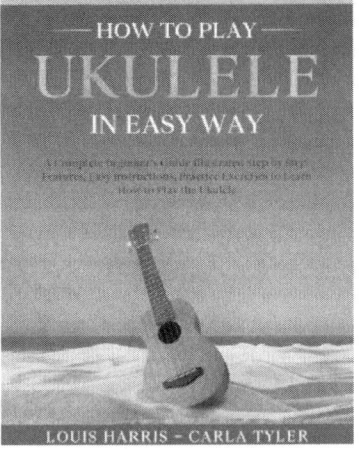

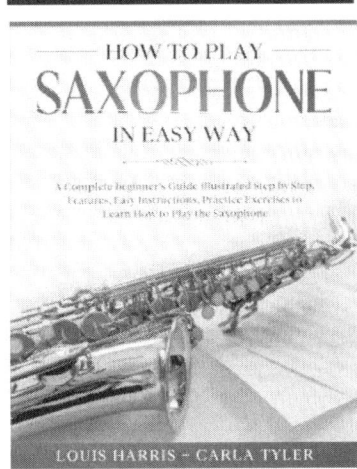

Search: "Louis Harris"

on Amazon

Kind reader,

Thank you very much, I hope you enjoyed the book.

Can I ask you a big favor?

I would be grateful if you would please take a few minutes to leave me a gold star on Amazon.

Thank you again for your support.

Louis Harris

Printed in Great Britain
by Amazon